CHRISTMAS
Puzzles

Written by Simon Tudhope
Designed by Sharon Cooper

Illustrated by
Sandra Aguilar, Helen Graper
and Mattia Cerato

The label machine is broken in Santa's workshop. Can you unscramble the letters to work out what each gift is?

EDYDT

KIEB

RINTA

KTASSE

BOTRO

ind Santa and Rudolph a route through the
ouds to the runway below.

In Santa's workshop, each elf can wrap 1 gift every 30 seconds. How many gifts can 5 elves wrap in 3 minutes? Write your anwer in the box below.

Gifts wrapped:

....

Wrapping Department

H	G	I	E	L	S	A	Y	O
O	N	S	R	U	E	Z	H	C
T	I	V	Y	O	B	G	E	S
A	K	G	S	C	I	W	N	T
L	C	M	O	F	D	R	X	A
E	O	V	R	T	E	E	K	B
N	T	O	A	Y	F	A	U	L
B	S	U	P	A	Q	T	S	E
T	I	Y	L	L	O	H	A	T

STOCKING   FROST   WREATH
FEAST   SLEIGH   STABLE
HOLLY   ANGEL   IVY

Which naughty elf pinched Frosty's nose?

MISSING!

FROSTY'S NOSE!

THE DAWN DODGER

THE DAWN DODGER

Find Nils a route across the ice so he can get a cup of hot chocolate.

Nils

HOT CHOCOLATE

HOT CHOCOLATE

The number on each decoration is the sum of the two hanging directly beneath it. Write the missing numbers on the blank decorations.

8

Yuri must collect all the reindeer so that Santa can deliver his presents. Find him a route that goes through each pen only once and finishes by Santa's sleigh.

Yuri

Mia is thinking of her ideal Christmas tree. Can you find it for her in this Christmas tree farm?

In each of these gifts, find a festive word that starts with the letter in the middle, and then circles clockwise or counter-clockwise around the gift.

a c r
l o

e l r i
a c
g n h o

Fill each grid with these four symbols. Each row, column and four-square block must contain one of each.

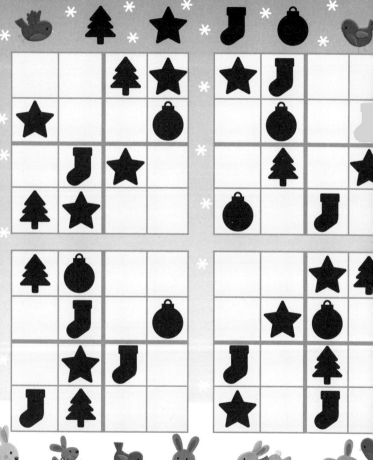

hich socket are the Christmas tree lights
ugged into?

Draw stripes on one-third of the cookies,
then add dots to 75% of those left blank.
How many plain cookies are left?

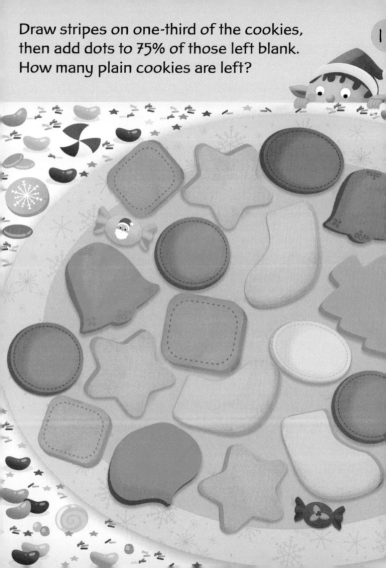

Can you find 2 decorations shaped like presents, 3 decorations shaped like birds, and 7 candy canes?

15

Which row of snowmen matches the silhouette?

acy and Dean are having a race. Count the
umber of seconds on each sign to find out
ho gets to the finish first.

17

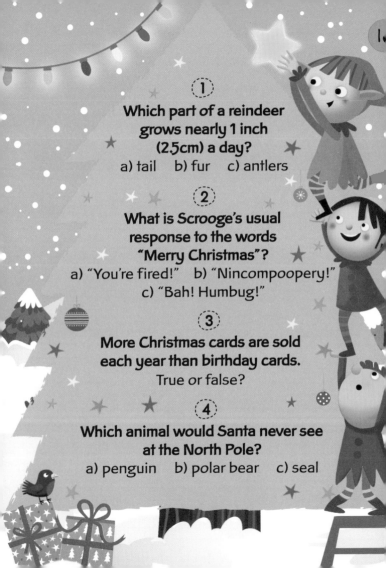

(1)
Which part of a reindeer grows nearly 1 inch (2.5cm) a day?
a) tail   b) fur   c) antlers

(2)
What is Scrooge's usual response to the words "Merry Christmas"?
a) "You're fired!"   b) "Nincompoopery!"
c) "Bah! Humbug!"

(3)
More Christmas cards are sold each year than birthday cards.
True or false?

(4)
Which animal would Santa never see at the North Pole?
a) penguin   b) polar bear   c) seal

ach snowman needs a hat and scarf, three uttons, two lumps of coal for eyes and a carrot r a nose. How many snowmen can Jo decorate om the assortment below?

19

Circle 8 differences between the pictures below.

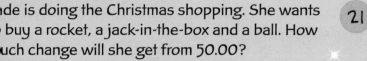

...de is doing the Christmas shopping. She wants
...o buy a rocket, a jack-in-the-box and a ball. How
...uch change will she get from 50.00?

Teddy
12.50

Rocket
14.00

Blocks
8.00

Car
12.50

Doll
15.00

ck-
the
ox
50

Robot
9.00

Ball

Dinosaur
10.50

5.50

Are there enough carrots for every reindeer to have one?

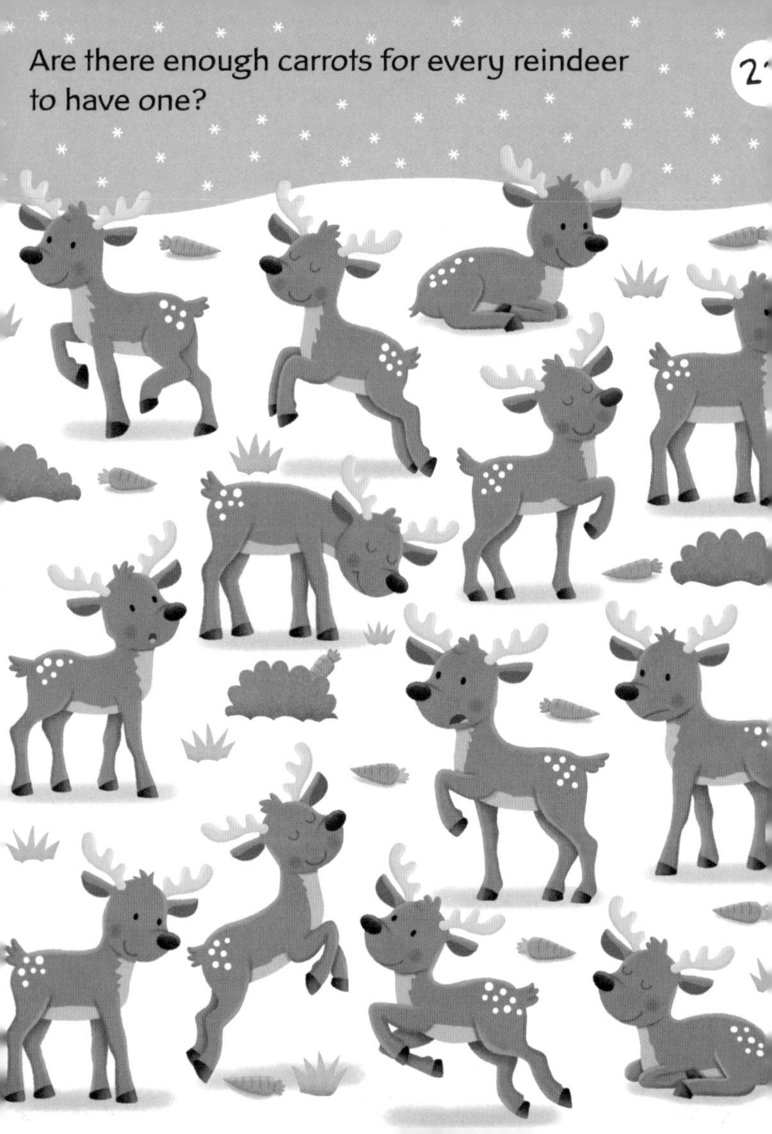

cross

Christmas songs (6)

It guided the Three Kings (4)

Santa's little helpers (5)

It carried Mary to Bethlehem (6)

Santa lives at the North _____ (4)

. Santa flies on it (6)

Down

1. The period leading up to Christmas (6)

3. The type of building Jesus was born in (6)

4. The leaves on a Christmas tree (7)

8. Rudolph's is red (4)

Are there enough snowballs for everyone to throw 5?

ome of these decorations are symmetrical.
hen you divide them in half with a straight line,
ch half is an exact reflection of the other. Can
ou find the decoration which isn't symmetrical?

Can you find the present that isn't one of a pair?

Santa's Grotto

Answers

Answer: BIKE, TEDDY, TRAIN, SKATES, ROBOT

Answer: 30 gifts wrapped

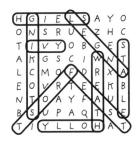

(5)

(6)

(7)

Answers

(8)

(11) Answer: CAROL, ANGEL, CHOIR

(12)

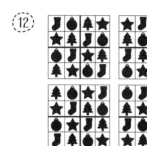

(9)

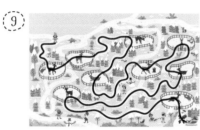

(13)

(10)

(14) Answer: 3 plain cookies (6 with stripes, 9 with dot...

Answers

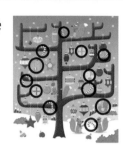

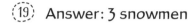

Answer: C

Answer: Macy wins
Dean = 33 seconds
Macy = 32 seconds

Answers:
1. c
2. c
3. false
4. a (Penguins don't live at the North Pole.)

(19) Answer: 3 snowmen

(20)

(21) Answer: 11.00

(22) Answer: No
13 reindeer
10 carrots

Answers

23

26

24

Answer: Yes
5 children
26 snowballs

25

Edited by Sam Taplin
Digital manipulation by Keith Furnival

First published in 2018 by Usborne Publishing Ltd. 83–85 Saffron Hill, London ECIN 8RT, England.
www.usborne.com © 2018 Usborne Publishing Ltd. The name Usborne and the devices ♀ 🐝 are Trade Marks
of Usborne Publishing Ltd.